Reformation

A PICTURE STORY OF

Martin Luther

by Dietrich Steinwede

Copyright © 1983, Fortress Press, Philadelphia

(additional publishing data, page 56)

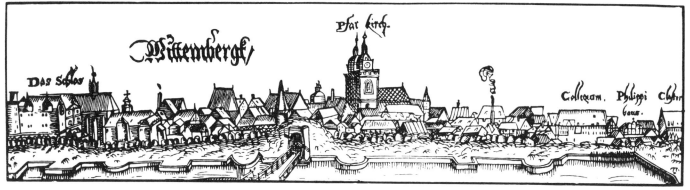

Wittenberg in the heart of Germany over 450 years ago
is a small city of about 2100 people.

Mid-sixteenth-century woodcut
by Lucas Cranach the Elder (or his workshop)

Martin Luther
is an Augustinian monk
in Wittenberg,
a priest,
Doctor of Theology,
and professor at the University.

Luther the monk
Color woodcut by Lucas Cranach 1520

2

Writing desk
Contemporary woodcut

Priest offering the sacrifice of the mass
before a portrait of Mary
Contemporary woodcut

Martin Luther is a busy man.
He works day and night studying the Bible.
He reads many books, even writes some of his own.
He seeks to get at the truth—
the truth about God and Jesus Christ.

As a priest, Luther says mass.
As a man, he suffers intense anxiety—
anxiety about his sins,
and about dying.
He is fearful of the punishment for sin
that awaits him when he dies—
the anguish of purgatory.

Many people in Luther's day are deathly afraid of an angry God.
They fear that God's dreadful judgment will come upon them at death,
and they will be cast into the jaws of hell
instead of being ushered into paradise, the eternal light of God's presence.

The Last Judgment consigns to eternal life
and eternal condemnation
Contemporary woodcut

The Four Horsemen of the Apocalypse
Woodcut by Albrecht Dürer 1497

And I saw, and behold, a white horse,
and its rider had a bow . . .
And out came another horse, bright red;
its rider was permitted
to take peace from the earth,
so that men should slay one another;
and he was given a great sword . . .
And I saw, and behold, a black horse,
and its rider had a balance in his hand . . .
And I saw, and behold, a pale horse,
and its rider's name was Death,
and Hades followed him;
and they were given power over a fourth of the earth,
to kill . . .

Revelation 6:2–8

It is an age of anxiety.
Fear stalks the land.

"The end of the world is at hand," they say,
"All will soon be over.
The scourges of the last days are upon us,
those fearful horsemen of Revelation.
They will cut down the mighty,
even pope and emperor,
as surely as the rest of us.
Not even the poor will escape."

Many fear for their health.
Sickness is everywhere,
plague sweeping the land—
especially the Black Death.

The people ask in alarm:
"What can we do?
How are we to be saved?"

Many pray to the saints.
They venerate the relics of the saints—
the bones and other sacred objects.

Many go on pilgrimage to holy places,
even the sick and the crippled
joining in their candlelight processions.

Many visit the "Schöne Maria,"
a shrine in the city of Regensburg.
Here they pray, sing hymns,
and call on the Blessed Virgin Mary.
Overwhelmed with anguish, pain, and despair,
they fling themselves at her feet,
begging for help.

The "Schöne Maria" shrine at Regensburg
Woodcut by Michael Ostendorfer about 1523

Sultan Suleiman II
Engraving by M. Lorch 1559

The people live in constant dread of powerful enemies,
especially the Ottoman Turks.
Led by their sultan, Suleiman the Magnificent,
the Turks are out to conquer all of Europe.

Occupied lands to the east
are being systematically ravaged and burned.
The Turks have already reached the outskirts of Vienna.
No wonder the people live in terror . . .

Martin Luther speaks of this peril later in one of his hymns:

Lord, keep us steadfast in thy Word
And curb the Turks' and papists' sword,
Who Jesus Christ, thine only Son,
Fain would tumble from off thy throne.

Turkish soldiers
looting and burning
Woodcut 1543

It is an age of terrible anxiety.
People are dreadfully afraid
of the punishments meted out by the courts.
Accused persons are often tortured
to exact a confession—which is
dutifully written down by a court clerk.
One form of torture is the "rack,"
powered by weights or a turning winch.
Another has the prisoner being "cooked"
inside a red-hot metal ox.

Women are burned as "witches"
simply because someone accuses them
or speaks evil of them.
The devil is pictured as a dragon
grabbing a "witch" by her hair,
while others are burned at the stake
or beheaded by the sword.
In 1484 a bull of Pope Innocent VIII
approved all manner of torture in
the persecution of witches.

Witch-burning at Derneburg
Woodcut 1555

7

But it is also a glorious time,
an age of new beginnings.
All over Europe strong rulers are in control.
In Germany Emperor Maximilian
is known as "the last of the knights."
In France King Francis I
is bent on conquering Italy.
In England King Henry VIII will eventually
establish a church of his own—
the so-called Anglican Church.

Right: Emperor Maximilian—portrait by Albrecht Dürer
Below left: King Francis I—portrait by Jean Clouet
Below right: King Henry VIII—portrait by Hans Holbein the Younger

It is a new and glorious age.
A man named Christopher Columbus
sails three ships westward across the ocean.
He believes that the earth is round
and that he can reach the Far East by sailing west.
Columbus discovers a brand-new continent—America.
He thinks he has reached India.
The "Indians" he encounters are a native people
previously unknown to the world of that time.

Ever since Columbus's discovery, people know that the earth is round.

Shortly afterwards another man,
the learned Nicolaus Copernicus,
begins to realize that the earth is not only spherical in shape;
it is also a planet which, with other planets, is orbiting the sun.
The center of things is the sun, not the earth.
This is what Copernicus will teach—
a very unsettling idea.

Actually this new understanding is still in the offing.
Just now, at the beginning of the sixteenth century,
most people believe what their forebears had always believed—
that the earth is a flat disk surrounded by an overarching firmament.
Beyond that firmament is water, and beyond that water the abode of God.
From high above, God reaches down
to embrace the whole world in his loving arms.
This is also how Martin Luther sees it.

Columbus landing in New Spain (Haiti)
Woodcut from the oldest account of
Columbus's journey, Basel 1494

Luther's picture of the world—
with God located beyond the firmament
Color woodcut from the Bible of Paul Eber 1565

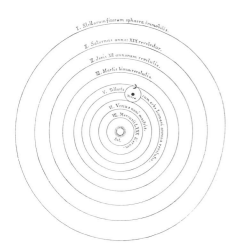

The Copernican world view—
with planet Earth orbiting the sun,
which is at the center of the whole system

Johannes Gutenberg—engraving 1584

Gutenberg had printed a beautiful Bible,
in many copies, with two columns of 42 lines on each sheet.
Large numbers of people can now buy and keep their own Bible.
The Bible need no longer be painstakingly copied by hand.
It can be printed—each copy is cheaper that way.

Large numbers of people can now buy and own books.
They read all sorts of books.
Every sizable city in Europe has its own print shop.
New books are continually being printed,
new black-and-white pictures too.

Printing and reading like that is unprecedented.
It is a revolutionary development.

Print shop—woodcut by J. Amman 1574

It is a new and glorious time like none preceding it.
At Mainz, only fifty years before Columbus's discovery,
Johannes Gutenberg had developed the art of printing.
Letters are now made by pouring hot lead into a mold.
These letters are then set into a tray in rows
in such a way as to form words and sentences.
The tray of lined-up letters is then inked
and pressed down hard on sheets of white paper
to make any desired number of copies of the whole page.

Thus from a single tray or frame many printed sheets are made.
The various sheets drawn from many frames
are then combined into a book.
The letters are movable. This means that
they can be taken out of any particular line or frame,
put into another, and used again.

It is also possible to print single sheets or flyers,
even black-and-white pictures,
and where the whole frame is carved by hand—a woodcut!

Merchant's warehouse—woodcut 1539

Jacob Fugger and his chief bookkeeper M. Schwarz.
Schwarz pictures himself with the world-famous banker-businessman
in a 1519 picture book about clothing.
Branch offices of the firm are named on the cabinet:
Rome, Venice, Budapest, Cracow;
Milan, Innsbruck, Nürnberg, Antwerp, Lisbon.

Something else is happening too.
In Europe there are now big business and commercial firms,
among them some powerful German merchants,
such as the Fuggers in Augsburg.
They buy and sell far and wide.

At first the Fuggers dealt in spices
together with silk and wool.
Now they also own mines.
Ore is taken from the earth
and smelted into iron, copper, silver, and lead.
Products of this kind are easy to sell.
They bring in money.

Their mines have made the Fuggers exceedingly rich.
Their firm has connections all over Europe.
They loan money, lots of it—even to the Emperor.
They get interest on the loans.

The Fuggers are a power to be reckoned with in Germany.

The papacy in Rome is a mighty power too.
This is the time of the Renaissance (a word that actually means "new birth"),
a time when human beings are rediscovering their own creativity.
In every area there are new beginnings.
It all started in Italy, where learning flourishes once again.
There is a rebirth of the arts—sculpture, painting, architecture.
Famous artists are at work in Rome,
many of them commissioned by the pope.
The ancient Church of St. Peter, a marvelous basilica begun by the
fourth-century emperor Constantine, is dismantled and rebuilt
in modern style—with a huge cupola.

Pope Leo X
Ornament from the June 15, 1520, papal bull—written
in Latin—that threatens Luther with excommunication

The pope imparts his blessing to the throng in St. Peter's Square.
Construction on the new cupola for St. Peter's Cathedral is further along
(in this 1550 engraving) than it was in 1517

Medallions from one of Hutten's writings 1523

This is the age of humanism.
A fresh appreciation of humanity
is spreading across Europe.
Humanistic studies are flourishing.
The freedom and dignity of human beings
again count for something,
as do reason and morality.
The humanists are rediscovering antiquity.
They say that the ancients, especially the Greeks,
were more humane than we are today. They begin to delve deeply
into ancient Greek philosophy and poetry.

Franz von Sickingen—engraving by D. Hopfer

Erasmus of Rotterdam, a humanist,
is a diligent student of the Bible.
"The New Testament was written in Greek," he says,
"and we ought to be reading it in its original language."
In 1516 Erasmus publishes the New Testament in Greek.

Another humanist is the knight Ulrich von Hutten.
He wears the laurel wreath of a poet.
Hutten is a zealous opponent of papal power,
and of the German princes.
He wants to reform the empire
and destroy the power of the princes.

A friend of his, Franz von Sickingen,
wages his own private war
against the archbishop of Trier.
The battle is lost when the knight
is mortally wounded in his own castle at Landstuhl.
Following the knight's death, Hutten too is obliged
to flee to Switzerland, where he dies in 1523.

The church is mightier than either knights or humanists because it holds the power of salvation. It issues indulgences—letters that reduce penalties the church has previously imposed on people for sins already forgiven. It sells them to people concerned about their soul's salvation.

The elector of Brandenburg (electors were powerful rulers who helped choose the next emperor) has a younger brother Albrecht. Using money borrowed from the Fuggers, Albrecht gained the approval of both pope and emperor to hold three major church offices at one time—in Halberstadt, Magdeburg, and Mainz. Now the loan has to be repaid.

Pope Leo X authorizes a special indulgence to help Archbishop Albrecht and names him commissioner of indulgences for all of Germany. Proceeds from the special sale will build St. Peter's Church in Rome—except that Albrecht is free to keep half the money for paying off his debts.

In 1515 Johann Tetzel, a Dominican named as assistant commissioner, boldly sets to work preaching indulgences. Wherever he goes to extract money from the people, he sets up in the churches his indulgence cross and a banner showing the pope's coat of arms with a money chest beside it.

With a perfectly straight face Tetzel preaches:
"As soon as the coin in the coffer rings,
the soul from purgatory springs."

In Ernestine (Electoral) Saxony, which includes the city of Wittenberg, Tetzel is forbidden to preach. Elector Frederick the Wise, Luther's ruler, will not allow it. His people, though, gladly travel to nearby Jüterbog just across the border in Brandenburg—to buy Tetzel's indulgences.

Above: Archbishop Albrecht—engraving by Albrecht Dürer
Below left: Johann Tetzel—seventeenth-century engraving
Below right: Fifteenth-century letter of indulgence

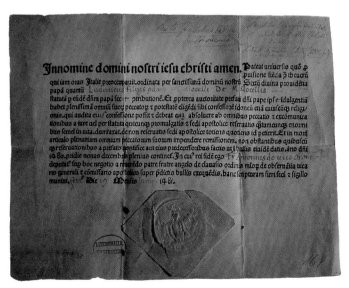

Martin Luther takes up the battle against indulgences.
A monk, Doctor of Theology, and professor at the University
of Wittenberg, Luther writes his *Ninety-five Theses*—in Latin—
and sends them to learned colleagues, priests, and bishops.
He sends a copy also to Archbishop Albrecht of Mainz—
along with a letter.
The date is October 31, 1517.

In his letter Luther says to the archbishop:
"What a danger for a bishop to permit the loud noise
of indulgences among his people, while the gospel
is silenced. If you take a look at my theses, you will
see how dubious is this belief concerning indulgences,
which these preachers propagate as if it were the
surest thing in the whole world. On no occasion has
Christ ordered that indulgences should be preached,
but he forcefully commanded the gospel to be preached."

Luther portrait 1519—from a contemporary account of the Leipzig Debate

Preaching indulgences in the church—contemporary woodcut

In his *Ninety-five Theses* Luther asserts:

1 When our Lord and Master Jesus Christ said, "Repent" [Matt. 4:17], he willed
the entire life of believers to be one of repentance.

11 Those tares of changing the canonical penalty to the penalty of purgatory were
evidently sown while the bishops slept [Matt. 13:25].

27 They preach only human doctrines who say that as soon as the money clinks
into the money chest, the soul flies out of purgatory.

36 Any truly repentant Christian has a right to full remission of penalty and guilt,
even without indulgence letters.

43 Christians are to be taught that he who gives to the poor or lends to the needy
does a better deed than he who buys indulgences.

62 The true treasure of the church is the most holy gospel of the glory and grace
of God.

79 To say that the cross emblazoned with the papal coat of arms, and set up by the
indulgence preachers, is equal in worth to the cross of Christ is blasphemy.

81 This unbridled preaching of indulgences makes it difficult even for learned men
to rescue the reverence which is due the pope from slander or from the shrewd
questions of the laity.

86 Such as: "Why does not the pope, whose wealth is today greater than the
wealth of the richest king, build this one basilica of St. Peter with his own
money rather than with the money of poor believers?"

Academic disputation—woodcut by Hans Burgkmair 1519

Luther says later concerning his Latin theses:
"I circulated my disputation notice to academics, inviting them
to discuss the issues with me."

What Luther envisions is a scholarly debate with his faculty
colleagues on the topic of indulgences.

But then a recipient of the theses has them published—
not in Latin but in German, the language of the common people.
Copies are soon circulating in every direction.
They spread like wildfire.
Within two weeks they are all over Germany.
People grab them wherever they can lay hands on them.
The theses are read avidly and discussed.

Many people had long been waiting for someone to speak out
against all that was evil and untrue in the church.
Now they welcome the theses: "It's finally happened.
Luther's our man!"

The impact of the theses is unbelievable. Luther says of it
later: "I was shocked myself to see the theses distributed all
over the country. It was by force of circumstances and through
no plan of mine that I got caught up in this whirlwind. God is
my witness that it was not of my choosing."

Only later did word get around that Luther had first posted his
theses on the door of the Castle Church in Wittenberg . . .

The Castle Church in Wittenberg, where the larger door (on the left)
served also as the university bulletin board.
The oldest extant representation of the Castle Church—by Lucas Cranach 1519

Luther wants to drive out indulgences the way Jesus drove the money-changers out of the temple. Lucas Cranach, Luther's famous painter-friend, illustrates that intention in a whole series of woodcuts, for which he provides accompanying texts:

Jesus found in the temple those who were selling
oxen and sheep and pigeons, and the money-changers.
And making a whip of cords, he drove them all out,
and he poured out the coins of the money-changers
and overturned their tables.
And he told those who sold the pigeons,
"Take these things away!
You shall not make my Father's house a house of trade.
You received everything freely. Therefore give freely.
Your money perish with you!"

Here sits the Antichrist in God's holy temple
overturning everything God had ordained.
He suppresses Holy Scripture
and sells remission of sins,
indulgences, and churchly offices.
He burdens consciences with his laws.
He declares sainthood for some
and condemns others unto the fourth generation.
He commands obedience to his own voice
as if it were the voice of God.

Woodcuts from the *Passional of Christ and Antichrist* by Lucas Cranach 1521

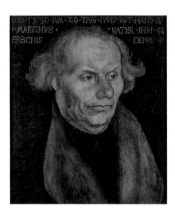

Luther's parents—portraits by Lucas Cranach 1527

Who is this Martin Luther who dares
to speak out against the church's indulgence preaching—
and thereby against the pope?
Everywhere people are wondering and asking:
Who is this man?
Where does he come from? Who are his parents?

Martin Luther was born November 10, 1483,
in the city of Eisleben in Thuringia.
His parents are Hans and Margarethe Luther.
Martin comes from a long line of peasants, tillers of the soil.
His father soon moves from Eisleben to Mansfeld
to find employment in the mines.
Hans rents a forge
where he can smelt copper ore into raw copper.
Operating the forge, he is in business for himself.
Later reports indicate that Martin's mother is
"a good woman with many fine qualities about her."

In Mansfeld the mines produce copper. The Saxony silver mine pictured here was painted around 1500 by Hans Hesse for St. Anne's Church in Annaberg in Saxony. The upper left portion of the picture tells the legend of the mine's origin. An angel appears to a mountain man in a dream and shows him a tree: "You are going to find a silver treasure." The mountaineer climbs the tree, thinking to pluck silver fruit from its branches. The angel then appears to him a second time: "Look down below, at the foot of the tree!" Then the mountain man begins to dig—and discovers silver ore.

Forge, of the kind used by Hans Luther—from "The Old Cemetery," a painting done as a memorial to the Stossnack family in Eisleben 1536

Martin starts school in Mansfeld,
attending later also in Magdeburg and in Eisenach.
In Magdeburg he goes up and down the streets
—as was the custom—
singing at each house and begging:
"A little bread for the love of God!"

One of the women of Eisenach is attracted to the boy.
Frau Cotta takes him into her own home.

Hans Luther wants his son to amount to something
so he sends Martin to Erfurt,
where the youth enrolls as a student at the university.

School—woodcut by J. Köbel 1524

University lecture—woodcut by Hans Burgkmair 1519

In 1501 Martin, like all other beginners enrolling at the
university, studies liberal arts. In 1502 he gets his
Bachelor's degree, in January of 1505 his Master of Arts.

A good student, Luther enjoys university life.
He is happy with his studies and happy spending time with his
friends. He loves music, especially playing the lute.

In May of 1505 Luther takes up the study of law—
to please his father.

Students in those days took an oath:

Do you solemnly promise to obey the rector?
Will you abide by the rules and regulations of the University?
Will you strive to improve it and be a credit to it?
If you step out of line, whether by laxity, disobedience,
or in any other way,
do you promise to heed the rector's command
and promptly leave school?
If so, swear it by God and the holy Evangelists!

A few months later, on July 2, 1505, after a brief visit at home with his parents, Luther leaves Mansfeld to hike back to the University. Near the village of Stotternheim, not far from Erfurt, he is caught in a severe thunderstorm.

A bolt of lightning strikes close by, knocking him to the ground. In terror he cries out to his father's favorite saint, the patroness of miners: "St. Anne, help me, and I will become a monk!"

St. Anne is the mother of the Virgin Mary, who is the mother of Jesus.

Luther keeps the promise he made in a moment of great fright. He quits his law studies. On July 15 he gathers his student friends together and tells them: "After today you'll not be seeing me. Tomorrow I'm entering the monastery to become a monk."

His stunned friends cannot dissuade him—his decision is final. The next morning they tearfully accompany him to the so-called Black Cloister of the Augustinian Hermits in Erfurt.

Luther is initiated into the order, first as a novice, then as a full-fledged monk. His head is shaven to give him the tonsure—a badge of membership in the order. He dons the traditional Augustinian garb, the black cowl with the large hood that is to be worn at all times, day and night. He adopts the prescribed customs and rituals—frequent praying and singing, fasting, prayers, and confessions, two meals a day. He lives in a tiny cell, furnished with only a bed, a table, and one chair. Silence is observed almost perpetually. Communication among the monks is by sign language. Luther cleans his own room, helps in the kitchen, and begs alms in the streets of Erfurt.

St. Anne holding Mary and the baby Jesus—sculpture from the Erfurt Cathedral about 1330

The city of Erfurt (at left the cathedral in which Luther is ordained a priest)—from Hartmann Schedel's History of the World 1493

Luther takes the monastic oath. Falling prostrate on the floor, he vows: "From henceforth I shall serve you God, you Jesus, you only."

The vow is regarded as a kind of baptism. Luther is said to be like a child who has been washed clean in the waters of baptism. He now leads a holy life, sober and sedate. He thinks constantly about his sins. He wonders: "How can I find a gracious God?"

Hans Luther is furious that his son should have become a monk.

On April 3, 1507, in the Erfurt Cathedral Luther is ordained to the priesthood. A month later he says his first mass. Luther's superiors, finding him to be exceedingly bright, assign him in 1508 to study theology at the recently founded University of Wittenberg. Here he is involved constantly in reading and studying the Bible. In the fall of 1509 he returns to Erfurt.

In 1510 the Augustinians send Luther on a long and difficult business trip to Rome. While there he rushes feverishly from church to church, praying in all the famous churches of Rome. He says of the experience later: "At the time, I was such a mad and arrogant saint that I believed all the stinking lies they had concocted." Then he returns to his monastery in Erfurt.

Luther as a monk—engraving by Lucas Cranach 1520

Piazza del Popolo in Rome. Adjacent to the church of Santa Maria del Popolo is the cloister of the Augustinian Hermits where Luther lives while he is in Rome—painting from the sixteenth century

In 1511 Johann von Staupitz, vicar-general of the Augustinians in Germany, arranges for Luther to enter the monastery in Wittenberg

Luther trusts Dr. Staupitz,
who had helped him often in his
moments of restlessness and deep despair:
"Look to the wounds of Christ," Staupitz used to say.
"Christ was speaking also of you when he said,
'No one will snatch you out of my hand.'"

Luther spends all his time studying.
He lectures at the university,
interpreting the Scriptures.
He preaches in the churches of Wittenberg,
putting his whole heart into every sermon.
The people hear him gladly.

In 1512 Luther earns his doctorate in theology.
He becomes a professor at the university
and lectures on various books of the Bible.
At the same time Luther wears himself out by
heaping heavy burdens on his conscience.
His sins torment him and will not let him go:
"How can I find a gracious God?"

Johann von Staupitz, vicar-general of the Augustinian Hermits in Germany
Sixteenth-century portrait from St. Peter's Abbey in Salzburg

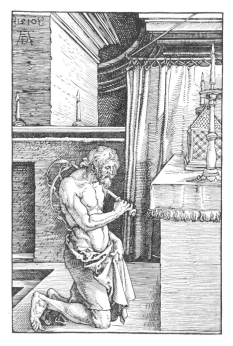

The penitent—
woodcut by
Albrecht Dürer 1510

Like a penitent who beats his back to a bloody pulp,
Luther punishes himself unmercifully.
His sins always loom so terribly large in his sight.
He torments himself endlessly—
until at last he makes a discovery,
a great and liberating discovery
in Romans 1:17: by grace alone . . .

Luther says of it later:

It is true that I was a devout monk and observed the rules of my order so rigidly that I can say: If any monk ever got to heaven through monkery, then I too should have made it. All my monastery companions who knew me will testify to that. In fact, if it had lasted much longer, I should have killed myself with vigils, praying, reading, and other labors.

With thee counts nothing but thy grace
To cover all our failing.
The best life cannot win the race,
Good works are unavailing.
Before thee no one glory can,
And so must tremble every man,
And live by thy grace only.

Luther in his Doctor's cap
Engraving by Lucas Cranach 1521

Later Luther will write these hymn stanzas:

Forlorn and lost in death I lay,
A captive to the devil,
My sin lay heavy, night and day,
For I was born in evil.
I fell but deeper for my strife,
There was no good in all my life,
For sin had all possessed me.

My good works they were worthless quite,
A mock was all my merit;
My will hated God's judging light,
To all good dead and buried.
E'en to despair me anguish bore,
That naught but death lay me before;
To hell I fast was sinking.

The pope and higher clergy
as "laborers in the vineyard" (Matthew 20).
Christ as Lord of the vineyard. Those
who labored longer also receive the promised wage,
nothing more. Painted by Lucas Cranach the
Younger in 1569 as a memorial to Paul Eber in the
City Church of Wittenberg (see also p. 48)

". . . live by thy grace only."
That is what Luther discovered:
"It depends not upon man's will or
exertion, but upon God's mercy"—
which is what Paul says in Romans 9:16.
In 1515–16 Luther lectured for a whole
year on Paul's Letter to the Romans.

"I get that from the Bible," says Luther.
"Faith tells it to me.
Jesus Christ tells it to me.
Everything depends on faith.
Everything depends on the grace of God.
It's all in the Bible, in Scripture.
Good works, veneration of the saints,
pilgrimages, relics—these are of no
value. They are worthless.
Jesus Christ alone is important.
Into him I am baptized.
On him I stake my life.
In him I will abide.
I can know.—I shall know nothing
but what my Lord Christ teaches me.
In this faith I will go to my grave."

The artist explains the picture above:

*The pope is thinking: We of the Roman church were first on the scene.
From the time of Peter we have been hard at work in God's vineyard.
We are bound to be well rewarded—certainly better than all who came later.
After all, we have worked longer and harder than they.*

*But no one receives more than any other. All receive the same reward—
one silver piece (symbol for the kingdom of God).*

*God is just. He pays what he promises.
Yet God rewards us in a way we least expect:
He rewards us out of his own great goodness and mercy—out of grace.*

By grace alone,
through faith alone,
through the Scriptures alone.
This is what Martin Luther discovered.
He never tires of repeating it.
The message is strange
to the church of his day.
It is a new doctrine.
The pope takes it to be directed against him.

And the pope responds.

In 1518 Cardinal Albrecht of Mainz lodges
an official complaint against Luther at Rome.
The proceedings that will determine his guilt
are placed in the hands of the Dominicans.
Pope Leo X calls Luther a "son of perdition,"
a "raging enemy of our salvation."

Luther is cited to appear before a tribunal of the Inquisition
in Rome. If he shows up there, he will of course be condemned,
possibly executed.

But it does not come to that.
Luther's sovereign Frederick the Wise, elector of Saxony,
decides to protect his university professor.
Because the pope is politically indebted to the elector,
Frederick is able to arrange for Luther's hearing to take place
in Augsburg before Cardinal Cajetan, an emissary of the pope.

Luther before Cajetan—color woodcut from the "Histories" of L. Rabus, Strassburg 1557

Luther arrives in Augsburg
and appears before Cardinal Cajetan.

"I was ordered," Luther recalls later, "to
take back what I had written in the theses,
those that he regarded as heretical."
Luther speaks boldly to the cardinal:
"You will have to prove my errors,
if any, from the Bible.
Give me solid reasons and I will recant.
Otherwise I can only insist
that the Holy Scriptures are supreme,
not the pope!"

At that the cardinal flies into a rage.
Luther has to flee the city.

25

Luther returns to Wittenberg.
The next summer, 1519, he travels to Leipzig
to accept the challenge of debate with
the learned theologian Dr. John Eck.
Their topic is the new faith, the "evangelical" faith
that comes from the evangel, the gospel.
Eck is a formidable defender of the old faith.
Luther is aided by Andrew Karlstadt, a professor of theology
at the University of Wittenberg who follows the new teaching.
The debate begins on the subject of indulgences.
Luther proposes the thesis:
"To say that indulgences are a blessing for a Christian
is insane, for they are in truth a hindrance to a good work; and
a Christian must reject indulgences because of their abuse."

They also debate whether the Roman church is supreme over all
others. Luther says: "The very feeble decrees of the Roman
pontiffs which have appeared in the last four hundred years
claim that the Roman church is superior to all others. Against
them stand the text of divine Scripture and the decree of the
Council of Nicaea." The debate lasts a long time and gets very
heated. It touches on the pope and whether he is capable of
error. It deals with councils and whether councils of the
church can err. Luther says: "Yes! The Roman church is not
superior to all other churches. The Roman church can err. A
council can err. The pope can err."

Because of his "evangelical" teachings a hundred years earlier,
Master John Huss of Bohemia had been burned at the stake by the
Council of Constance. He too would not take back what he had
written—unless convinced from the Bible that he was wrong. For
Huss too the Bible is the only norm for Christian faith and life.
Huss too had insisted that a council can err.

In his debate with John Eck Luther openly admits:
"Among the articles of John Huss I find many which are plainly
Christian and evangelical."

That is all the opponents need to hear. Following the debate Eck
hurries to Rome. He begins to devote himself to the task of
having Luther excommunicated—put out of the church.

The burning of John Huss by the Council of Constance 1415.
The miter's inscription, part of the mockery, reads *Heresiarcha*—heretic.
Engulfed in flames, Huss cries out:
"Jesus Christ, Son of the living God, have mercy on me."
Color woodcut from the Richenthal History of the Council of Constance

On June 15, 1520, Pope Leo X issues his bull
threatening Luther with excommunication.
He gives Luther sixty days in which to
take back everything he has written—
or fall under the ban of the church.

The bull requires everybody who can lay hands
on the writings of Luther to burn them.
The burning of his books begins
at Lüttich and Mainz and Cologne.

The bull includes the pope's own prayer to God:
"Arise, O Lord, and judge thy cause,
for foxes have risen up
to lay waste your vineyard."

The reference is to Luther.
The prayer pictures him as a cunning beast
out to destroy God's vineyard.

Burning Luther's books.
Frontispiece from Ulrich von Hutten's protest *Against
the Burning of Luther's Books at Mainz*
Woodcut 1520

Title page of the papal bull
in its German version
Woodcut 1520

Luther burns the papal bull
Color woodcut from the "Histories" of L. Rabus, Strassburg 1557

On December 10, 1520, Luther sends a signal of his own.
At Wittenberg's Elster gate he burns not only the papal bull
but also the papal laws and constitutions, the decretals.

An invitation had gone out to everyone in Wittenberg
who cherishes the evangelical faith.
Students and other townspeople join Luther at the fire.

As Luther flings the papal bull into the flames he says:
"As you [Pope Leo] have destroyed the Christ of God,
so let eternal fire destroy and consume you."

The burning signifies a final break with the Roman church.
A single individual stands up to the power of an institution
fifteen hundred years old.
But Luther does not flinch. He already has many followers.

On January 3, 1521, the church proclaims its ban
against the Augustinian monk of Wittenberg.
Many people in Germany are incensed by the action.

In the months just before the burning of the papal bull, Luther had published three treatises of fundamental importance for the Reformation.

August 1520
To the Christian Nobility of the German Nation Concerning the Reform of the Christian Estate

October 1520
The Babylonian Captivity of the Church

November 1520
The Freedom of a Christian

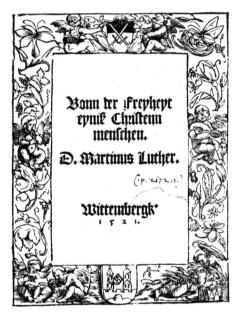

Title pages of Luther's Reformation writings—woodcuts 1520

All Christians are truly of the spiritual estate, and there is no difference among them. . . .
This is because we all have one baptism, one gospel, one faith . . . we are all consecrated priests through baptism . . . yes, we are all priests.

Fundamentally all of us Christians, both priests and laity, are equally priests . . . we have the same power in respect to the Word and the sacraments.
For we have received mercy not through our doings but through God's free promise and gift.

A Christian is a perfectly free Lord of all, subject to none.
A Christian is a perfectly dutiful servant of all, subject to all.
If the Son makes you free, you will be free indeed (John 8:36).

Luther's books spread like wildfire. Many people follow his lead in breaking with Rome.

Emperor Charles V – portrait by Barent van Orley, 1521

Beginning in 1519
the Holy Roman Empire of the German Nation
has a new emperor—
Charles V, of the house of Hapsburg.
A Spaniard, Charles is ruler of Spain and the New World
as well as of the Low Countries and Germany.
He speaks no German.

In the spring of 1521,
at the urging of Elector Frederick the Wise,
Charles V invites the monk Martin Luther of Wittenberg
to come to the city of Worms on the Rhine River
in order to appear before the Diet or parliament
of the German princes (nobility) and estates (imperial cities).
The emperor assures Luther that he will be safe.

*As we, and the estates of the Holy Empire, here assembled, have
undertaken and decreed to obtain information about certain doctrines and
certain books which formerly originated with you, we have given you and
hereby send our and the Empire's free safe-conduct to come hither and to
return hence. We desire you to prepare certainly to be here within twenty-
one days, relying on our safe-conduct and not fearing any violence.*

From the summons

The imperial summons (at right the signature of Archbishop Albrecht)

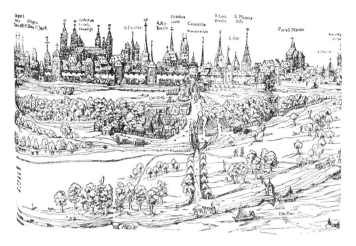

The city of Worms—woodcut from the Cosmography of Sebastian Münster 1556

Martin Luther travels to Worms
accompanied by the imperial herald Caspar Sturm.
Along the way he is greeted triumphantly
by the people of Leipzig, Naumburg, and Weimar.
In Erfurt he preaches to the Augustinians.
He passes through Eisenach, Hersfeld, and Frankfurt.
A letter reaches him from Worms, from his friend
George Spalatin, secretary to Frederick the Wise:
"Are you crazy, Martin? Turn back! Your life is in danger!"
But Luther says: "Even though there should be as many devils
in Worms as shingles on the roof, I would still enter."
"I was not afraid," Luther explained later. "God can
make a person that crazy."

Luther enters Worms on April 16. Huge crowds line the streets to catch a glimpse of the Wittenberg monk who dares to tangle with pope and emperor. Once settled in his assigned quarters, many friends come to visit him. On April 17 he is led secretly into the bishop's palace to appear before the Diet. He is told to take back all that he had written. He asks for time to consider the matter. The emperor gives him until the next day to think it over. Luther spends the night in prayer.

On April 18 Luther stands again before the emperor and the Diet—6 electors, 24 dukes, 7 margraves, 30 bishops, plus knights and emissaries of the imperial cities. The pageantry is impressive. There is not a vacant seat in the large hall. The sun has already set and the stuffy room is dark except for the burning candles. Once more the spokesman for the Diet puts the question: "Will you recant?" This time Luther answers. His speech is clear and strong, polite but determined. He says his books are of three kinds. He details the reasons why he cannot take back what he has written—unless someone will prove him to be in error.

He then repeats everything he had said—this time in Latin for the benefit of the dignitaries from Spain and Burgundy. It is a long speech. Luther is then admonished to make his answer brief and to the point. He does:

Unless I am convinced by the testimony of the Scriptures or by clear reason (for I do not trust either in the pope or in councils alone, since it is well known that they have often erred and contradicted themselves), I am bound by the Scriptures I have quoted and my conscience is captive to the Word of God. I cannot and I will not retract anything, since it is neither safe nor right to go against conscience. May God help me. Amen.

At that point the emperor adjourns the meeting. Luther's fate is sealed.

Luther before the Diet—color woodcut from the "Histories" of L. Rabus, Strassburg 1557

A few days later Luther stands before a committee of the Diet.
The archbishop of Trier states their case: "Don't you
see what you're doing? It can only lead to an uprising.
You'll split the nation apart. It's time to bend a little."
Luther stands firm: "For me, Scripture is all that counts.
In matters of faith each one must decide."

A message from the emperor arrives:
"You are to leave Worms—before the twenty-one days are up."
On April 26 Luther departs. He is in real danger:
the decision of the Diet is soon to be announced—
it will declare him an outlaw.
This is exactly what happens in the Edict of Worms,
issued against the Wittenberg monk by Emperor Charles V:

We declare Martin Luther to be an avowed heretic, no longer a member of God's church. We command all of you and each person individually not to house, lodge, or shelter him; not to offer food and drink to him, neither by words or deeds privately or publicly to offer him any help, devotion, aid, or assistance but that wherever you find or meet or are able to seize him, you make him your prisoner, send him to us under guard. . . . Furthermore, we command . . . that no person is to buy, sell, read, possess, copy, print, or allow to be copied or printed any writings . . . of the above-named Martin Luther . . . ; and that no one is to fall prey to his ideas, nor believe, preach, or defend them . . .

From the Edict of Worms, May 26, 1521

But Elector Frederick the Wise does not stand idly by. In a mock attack and "capture" he has Luther taken into protective custody and hurries him off to the Wartburg Castle in Thuringia. His deception is so successful that many of Luther's followers do not know of the Reformer's whereabouts. Albrecht Dürer, the famous artist, has this entry in his diary for 1521:

O God, if Luther is dead, who will henceforth explain to us the gospel? What might he not have written for us in the next ten or twenty years . . .

Luther, of course, was aware of his protector's plan. In a letter to Lucas Cranach on April 28, 1521, he writes:

Dear fellow-godfather Lucas: . . . I shall submit to being "imprisoned" and hidden away, though as yet I do not know where. I would have preferred to suffer death at the hands of the tyrants, especially those of the furious Duke George of Saxony, but I must not disregard the counsel of good men; I will await his appointed time . . .

From the Wartburg on May 14, 1521, Luther writes to Spalatin:

After being captured I was stripped of my own clothes and dressed in a knight's cloak. I am letting my hair and beard grow so that you would hardly know me. . . . Now I am living in Christian liberty.

Luther as Knight George—woodcut by Hans Sebald Beham

Luther is now known as "Knight George." He remains in hiding at the Wartburg for almost a year, until March 1522. But he makes good use of the time. Many writings emerge during this period of enforced solitude and idleness. The project that excites him more than any other is his translation of the Bible into the language of his people. He begins by translating the New Testament.

Luther wants the Word of God to be accessible to every German who can read, including workers and peasants, not just priests and scholars who know Latin. Others before him had translated the Latin Bible into German, but Luther translates directly from the Greek, the language in which the New Testament was originally written. That makes his translation totally new. It is so vivid and powerful that it becomes a standard for the whole German language. This German New Testament is published in September of 1522 as the "September Testament." Luther says later about the task of translating:

We do not have to inquire of the literal Latin, how we are to speak German. . . . Rather we must inquire about this of the mother in the home, the children on the street, the common man in the marketplace. We must be guided by their language, the way they speak, and do our translating accordingly.

His Preface to the "September Testament" includes these words:

Evangelium (gospel) is a Greek word and means in Greek a good message, good tidings, good news, a good report, which one sings and tells with gladness.

But things are not quiet for long at the Wartburg. Disturbing news comes out of Wittenberg that Andrew Karlstadt, Luther's colleague at the university, is trying to advance Luther's cause by violent means. "With Luther away," he says, "we have to do something!" Karlstadt rages against the monasteries and monastic life: "What good is it? Monastic practices are of no value whatever. That's what Luther said." Karlstadt rages against the sacrifice of the mass, against the transubstantiation of the bread and wine into the body and blood of Christ. He turns the Latin mass into a German worship service.

Image breaking, with a graphic illustration of Matt. 7:3 in the background—woodcut by E. Schon about 1530

In the Lord's Supper Karlstadt distributes wine as well as bread. Worshipers take the cup into their own hands. Karlstadt preaches: "Images are of the devil: Pray to God, not to statues of the saints!"

On December 3 radical students wreak havoc in the City Church, smashing statues, burning works of art. Even the image of the crucified Christ is not spared.

On December 4 Luther slips back into Wittenberg to quell the disturbances. An outlaw, he cannot stay long. Back in the Wartburg he promptly writes *A Sincere Admonition by Martin Luther to All Christians to Guard Against Insurrection and Rebellion:* "Those who read and rightly understand my teaching will not start an insurrection; they have not learned that from me!"

Luther's admonition is in vain. "Fanatics" arrive in Wittenberg claiming to be illuminated from within by the Spirit of God. They speak against Bible, preaching, and theology. Luther's friend Philip Melanchthon, professor of classical languages at the university, is appalled. But Karlstadt sides with the "prophets," telling his students to leave the university. Confusion mounts. The city council decides to call Luther back from exile. Elector Frederick disagrees: "I'll be unable to protect a man who has been excommunicated and outlawed." Luther comes anyway. On March 5, 1522, he writes to Elector Frederick from Borna: "I am going to Wittenberg under a far higher protection than the Elector's."

Back in monastic garb and tonsure, Luther mounts the pulpit of the City Church and preaches eight sermons in as many days: "Do not be misled. Violence is not the way! The Word alone! Jesus Christ alone! The cause is right, but don't hurry things. We must act in love, not haste. I will preach and write, but I will compel no one by force. Faith has to be accepted voluntarily."

And the miracle happens! Calm returns to Wittenberg and the fanatics disappear—all by the Word alone.

The older Karlstadt—seventeenth-century engraving

Luther preaches Christ crucified: "In him alone is the true theology and knowledge of God." Predella from Lucas Cranach's altar in the City Church of Wittenberg 1547. Cranach himself is pictured with a long beard, his fingers pointing downward toward Luther's wife Catherine, whose right hand rests on the arm of their son Hans.

Don't hurry things! Luther too, however, preaches that all Christians should receive the cup as well as the bread in Holy Communion. Christ himself had said: "Drink of it, *all* of you" (Matt. 26:27). Luther teaches that under the bread and wine the true body and blood of Christ are present. This reception of "both kinds" in the sacrament is pictured below by Lucas Cranach the Younger. He also pictures Luther's preaching of the crucified Christ, in whose name alone is our salvation (Acts 4:12). Beneath the pulpit is Elector Frederick the Wise bearing the cross.

Luther's baptismal preaching too is portrayed: When God's Word (the open Bible) is added, the water becomes a "water of God": "He who believes and is baptized will be saved" (Mark 16:16). Luther teaches infant baptism: "Bring the child to baptism with the prayer that God will grant him the gift of faith." Other reformers assert that no one can be baptized unless he is old enough to make confession for himself: "It is false and un-Christian to baptize little ones who do not understand." Luther opposes the rebaptizers.

By 1534 the anabaptists come to power in the city of Münster, their "new Jerusalem." Münster's first anabaptist mayor, Knipperdolling, wants to use force to usher in the "kingdom of God," including polygamy and communal ownership of property. In 1535 the bishop of Münster retakes the city and puts the anabaptists to death.

IN·RI

Trincket alle daraus.
Matthe. 26.

Alle Prophe
ten zeugen von
diesem/dz kein
ander name un
ter dem himel
sey. Act. 4.10.

Meanwhile Luther continues to fault Roman church practices. In the very same picture, Cranach presents a caricature of everything Luther has been opposing: the selling of indulgences, papal greed, incensation, votive candles, processions, veneration of the saints (see the processional banner), and the sacrifice of the mass. Holiness clearly does not consist in such external things as surplice, cassock, and tonsure. Cranach is exceedingly hard on the vain and unprofitable life of the monks: dice and playing cards are seen falling out of one monk's cowl; another waving his censer is fitted with a grotesque mask; the devil himself uses a bellows to put ungodly words into the ear of another monk preaching from the pulpit.

Two kinds of preaching
Color woodcut by Lucas
Cranach the Younger

Luther triggers immense unrest throughout the land. The unity of the faith is broken. Monks and nuns in their cloisters begin to call in question everything they had once cherished and revered. Some do so secretly, others openly; some just to stir up trouble, others to be true to their conscience. Some take up a secular occupation as a cobbler, baker, or carpenter. Others take up a "Lutheran" way of life, becoming preachers of the gospel. Some monasteries and convents stand empty after all their people leave. Many monks and nuns know *The Judgment of Martin Luther on Monastic Vows,* which he had written while still confined at the Wartburg in 1521. Some of them continue in the cloistered life of humility, poverty, piety, and devotion—confident that even in the cloister one can proclaim the Word of God.

Marriage of bishops and monks with nuns
Frontispiece of a pamphlet put out by the Franciscan Eberlin von Günzberg
Woodcut 1522

Beginning already in the spring of 1521 cloistered people were entering into marriage, either with people from outside or with other monks or nuns. On June 13, 1525, the former Augustinian monk Martin Luther and the former Cistercian nun Catherine von Bora are married.

In all, six children are born into the Luther family—three sons and three daughters. Luther now learns what it means to make beds, rock the cradle, change diapers, bind wounds, and wash soiled clothes.

Luther and Catherine von Bora—portraits by Lucas Cranach 1526

Later in life Luther says:

Who would ever have predicted it,
who would have read it in the stars—
that I would one day cause such heartache to my father,
get into such a scrape with the pope,
and marry an ex-nun?

From Luther's *Table Talk*

All over Europe the peasants are in a state of unrest. The pot, long simmering, is ready to boil over. Why?

Wealthy landholders among the nobility and clergy are exacting high rents from their tenants. Peasants deliver the tithe—a tenth of their crops—to the owners. They also render service, some in the role of serfs who belong to their masters body and soul. Even freeholders among the peasants are not permitted to hunt the woods or fish the waters where they live. Only the landowners have such rights. Animals can eat up the peasants' crops, and hunters trample their fields—the peasants have no recourse.

The peasants say things have to change. Does government always have to be in the hands of nobles and princes, abbots and bishops? "From Eden all aristocrats were banned, while Eve spun wool and Adam tilled the land."

Secret associations spring up. Members swear allegiance to the group. The *Bundschuh* is named for the leather thong *(Bund)* with which the peasant sandal *(Schuh)* was laced. But wherever peasant uprisings occur, they are quickly put down. In southwestern Germany Joss Fritz repeatedly calls on the peasants: "March with God, with the Crucified One, against the unjust landlords!" The peasant's laced shoe is a common symbol—along with the farmer's rake.

The Bundschuh banner shows the cross of Christ atop the peasant's shoe, a peasant kneeling alongside. In the foreground peasants take their oath of allegiance on the rake. In the background the sacrifice of Isaac symbolizes liberation, the angel's intervention showing God's opposition to the powerful making sacrificial lambs out of the weak. Peasants nearby gather hay with their rakes. Their only goal is to harvest their crops in peace—frontispiece from the pamphlet *The Bundschuh* 1513

The great reversal
Woodcut 1508

Radical ideas are taking hold:
"What might it be like if the church were turned upside down,
so that peasants would say mass
while nobles guided the plow
and monks led the horses?
That would be a switch!"
Pamphlets suggesting just that begin to make the rounds.

In 1524 the peasants of southwestern Germany go into action.
Peasant armies begin to march on the nobles,
besieging forts and castles,
attacking even the cloisters.
They have read Luther's ringing words
that a Christian is a free man.
They are Christians. They want to be free.
They put their hope in Martin Luther.

"The true, main, and basic articles
which all the peasants and tenants have
against the spiritual and temporal
authorities who are oppressing them"
Frontispiece to the 1525 edition of *The
Twelve Articles*

Peasant armies on the march with
weapons and gear in southern Germany
Woodcut 1522

In 1525 peasant armies with swords and spears are on the march in many places—in Swabia, Franconia, Thuringia, and elsewhere. Sebastian Lotzer, a Memmingen furrier with the Baltingen peasant army, formulates twelve articles listing the peasants' modest demands, among them the following:

• We are free—it says so in the Scriptures. And free we will be!
• In our congregations we want to choose our own pastors, people who will preach the pure gospel.
• The rents charged us are in many instances too high.
• We are willing to pay the tithe of our grain, but not of our cattle.
• We want the same freedom to catch wild game and fresh-water fish as our rulers enjoy.
• When we are accused of wrongdoing we want to be tried according to ancient written law, not according to the current whim of any overlord.
• And if anything in these articles is contrary to God's Word, we want it to be disregarded . . .

"The gospel of Jesus Christ," say the peasants, "is our constitution." Martin Luther writes his *Admonition to Peace: A Reply to the Twelve Articles of the Peasants in Swabia.* "You peasants," he says, "must be prepared to suffer grievous injustices without resorting to violence. You princes and lords, though, must quit oppressing the peasants and violating their rights." I would gladly risk my life, says Luther, to visit the peasants in Thuringia and in the Harz Mountains in order to explain my views and try to head off the impending bloodbath. His hopes are not realized.

The peasants have some outstanding leaders, including Wendel Hipler, former chancellor to the house of Hohenlohe, and the knight Florian Geyer. But they also have some radical leaders who exploit the peasants' deep anger and hatred toward the authorities, forgetting that violence can do no good.

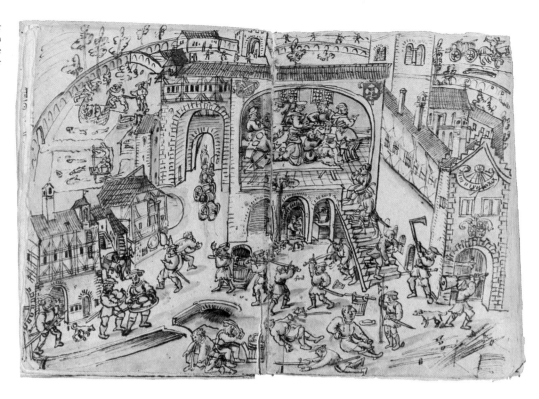

Peasants loot the Weissenau Cloister
in Upper Swabia
Color sketch from the
History of the Cloister

Thomas Münzer—1608 engraving based on a woodcut
by Christian von Sichem about 1524

At Weinsberg in Swabia, in the absence of more moderate leaders, the ruthless peasant chieftain Jäcklein Rohrbach leads a successful assault on the castle of Count Ludwig von Helfenstein. The count, Emperor Maximilian's own son-in-law, is captured and forced to run a gauntlet of peasants. Along with other nobles he dies an ignoble death.

In Thuringia Thomas Münzer stokes the fires of unrest. Eloquent as a preacher at Allstedt and a zealous theologian, Münzer is also a revolutionary, a fighter for justice who regards himself as a "servant of God against the godless." "I can't help but foment rebellion," he says. "The impoverished peasants already see it coming. Our lords and princes are a pack of thieves. They think they own everybody. They claim that the poor must submit to being fleeced by the tyrants. Not so—those who are mighty in lands and power will finally be forsaken by God. All property is to be held in common and distributed according to need. Any prince, count, or master who refuses to go along, even after being admonished, is to be hanged or beheaded."

Around the end of April 1525, Münzer and the preacher Henry Pfeiffer lead an army of peasants from Mühlhausen to attack the princes of Thuringia. In a matter of days they lay waste forty cloisters and many castles. "Press on, press on," Münzer writes to the miners of Mansfeld, "press on while the fire is hot. Let not your blades grow cold." The princes, however, led by John of Saxony (son of the now-deceased Frederick the Wise) and Philip of Hesse, destroy Münzer's peasant army at Frankenhausen in Thuringia. Münzer flees and hides out, but is found, tortured, and executed.

Peasants led away as prisoners
Contemporary woodcut

After the war the peasants reassemble at the Weissenau
Cloister, this time to swear allegiance once again. One
of the overlords, at the abbot's left elbow, reads aloud
the terms of the arrangement being renewed
Color sketch from the History of the Cloister

As in Thuringia, so also in Alsace, Franconia, and elsewhere the nobles fight back. One after another the peasant armies are crushed. The peasants never had been united; without a common leader they never could get together.

In Swabia the "Swabian League" of princes and abbots sends an army of professional mercenaries to engage the peasants. Under George Truchsess they stop the rebellion dead in its tracks, burning whole villages and slaughtering peasants by the thousands. Jäcklein Rohrbach is seized and suffers a hideous death. Escaped peasants are tracked down and beheaded. Some have their hands severed. Others are blinded.

Appalled by the deeds the peasants had earlier been committing, Luther had finally written *Against the Robbing and Murdering Hordes of Peasants:* "The authorities are to proceed against the peasants, with the sword if necessary. . . . Rebellion is like a great fire that can devastate a whole land, fill it with murder and bloodshed, make widows and orphans, and destroy everything."

The Peasants' Revolt is at an end. Peasants still alive must again swear allegiance to their landlords. They must again pay taxes and deliver the tithes. They must render service as in the past—and turn in their weapons.

The peasants are now oppressed as never before.

Luther sees help from the princes as essential for structuring the congregations. In 1525 he writes to his sovereign, Elector John:

Everywhere the parishes are in such poor condition. No one contributes anything. . . . The common man pays so little attention and respect to preachers and pastors that in a short time there will not be a parsonage, a school, or a pulpit functioning, and thus God's Word and worship will perish unless your Electoral Grace passes strict laws and carefully regulates the maintenance of parishes and pulpits. . . . Your Electoral Grace will certainly find means to deal with this situation. There are enough monasteries, collegiate chapters, benefices, endowments, and other similar things that can be used for this purpose, if only your Electoral Grace will issue an order.

The evangelical princes set up territorial churches, each prince himself serving as a kind of interim bishop. They take over properties that formerly belonged to the church. Congregations retain the right—so cherished by the peasants—to call their own evangelical pastors and preachers.

In 1526 at the first Diet of Speyer the princes decide that on religious issues each ruler will act "as he would hope to answer for it before God and the emperor."

In 1529 at the second Diet of Speyer the "Catholic" party wants to rescind the 1526 decision and enforce the 1521 Edict of Worms against Luther. Six "Evangelical" princes and fourteen imperial cities protest:

These are things that concern the glory of God and the welfare and salvation of every one of us; as to them, by the command of God, for the sake of our consciences, we are . . . bound to hold before all our Lord and God as highest King and Lord of Lords . . . we herewith protest and testify openly before God, that we consider null and void this decree of the Diet.

The protesting princes and imperial cities quit the meeting. From that time on, advocates of the new evangelical faith are called "Protestants."

Reformers and princes with Christ at the Last Supper (receiving bread *and* wine). A 1565 painting in the Castle Church at Dessau shows how the Reformation was associated with territorial rulers. At Jesus' right hand are Prince George of Anhalt, then Martin Luther; at Jesus' left hand, Melanchthon. In the left foreground is Prince John of Anhalt; in the right foreground, serving wine, is the painter himself, Lucas Cranach the Younger

In 1530 Emperor Charles V issues a conciliatory sounding call for a Diet to meet in Augsburg. He promises to "hear and consider in love and kindly concern the opinions of all parties." The Protestants draw up a statement to present to the Diet—the "Augsburg Confession."

Its author is Philip Melanchthon, professor of classical languages at Wittenberg and a friend of Luther. Melanchthon would like to heal the rift with the Roman church.

Officially Luther is still an outlaw, exiled from both church and state. He cannot attend the Diet, but he follows the proceedings as faithfully as possible from his refuge at the Coburg Castle. Messengers scurry back and forth with his mail. Luther encourages Melanchthon to be strong in faith and speak up for the gospel.

On July 25 it is a hot afternoon in Augsburg. The great hall of the bishop's palace is jammed with electors, princes, emissaries of the imperial cities, and other dignitaries. The chancellors of Electoral Saxony and of Ducal Saxony both stand before the emperor, the former holding the German version of the Confession, the latter the Latin version. The emperor wants to hear the Latin version. Elector John of Saxony insists that the German be read. His chancellor Christian Beyer reads the Augsburg Confession in a loud and clear German that carries right through the open windows to the anxious crowds outside.

Philip Melanchthon, author of the Augsburg Confession—engraving by Albrecht Dürer

The Diet of Augsburg—contemporary woodcut

The Augsburg Confession contains 28 articles, 22 of them about faith and doctrine. It asserts that the evangelical faith comes from the Scriptures and early church—and is not heresy.

Chancellor Beyer reads on and on while the emperor occasionally dozes. Many of the Catholic princes are amazed at what they hear. The bishop of Augsburg admits: "What the Lutherans say here is true. It is the pure truth. There's no denying it."

The emperor nonetheless commissions Dr. Eck to draft a rebuttal, which is then read to the Diet on August 3. The emperor declares Eck's statement to be the truth, but the evangelical princes refuse to concede. Led by Elector John of Saxony (nicknamed the Constant), Landgrave Philip of Hesse, Duke Ernest of Braunschweig-Lüneberg, and Margrave George of Brandenburg-Ansbach, they leave Augsburg when an unfavorable decision by the Diet seems imminent. In December of 1530 the evangelical princes gather in the town of Schmalkalden on the edge of the Thuringian Forest to discuss the situation. Emperor Charles V is determined to implement the decisions of Worms, by force if necessary. In March of 1531 seven evangelical princes conclude a defensive alliance against the emperor—the Schmalkald League.

The emperor, however, is in no position to move against them. With the Turks at the gates of Vienna, the empire itself is in peril of its life. The emperor needs the evangelical princes in his efforts to repulse the Turks. In 1532 he concludes a truce with the princes and from that time on the evangelical faith can begin to spread.

Talk now increases about the possibility of a great Christian council in which Protestants too would take part, one that could lead to fresh beginnings. In 1537 Pope Paul III actually calls such a council—to meet in Mantua—but the meeting never takes place.

At the request of his elector John Frederick (successor to John the Constant) Luther makes ready for the council. He writes a fresh summary of the evangelical faith, this time in even clearer form—the Schmalkald Articles.

In many quarters lively efforts are being made to bring Protestant and Catholic Christians together again. Emperor Charles V strongly encourages such moves. Many Protestants feel the rift could be healed if only the pope would allow priests to marry and the laity to receive the sacrament in "both kinds."

Conversations on religious unity are arranged in various places—in Hagenau (Alsace), Worms, Regensburg—but by 1541 there is still no progess in that direction. Protestants insist on holding to their evangelical faith—faith in the Christ who was baptized by John in the Jordan River—by grace alone, through Scripture alone, through faith alone.

Reformers at the Baptism of Jesus—painting by Lucas Cranach the Younger 1565

Choir of the Reformation period—mid-sixteenth-century woodcut

In Lutheran areas the hymns of the Reformation are being sung in every square, on every street corner. An enemy of the Reformation says later: "Luther's hymns have led more souls to perdition than all his books and sermons."

The new church will be a singing church.

"I would like to see all the arts, especially music, used in the service of the One who created them and gave them to us," says Luther. "If I had my way, children would learn not only languages and history but also singing and music." "Singing is the best skill and exercise there is," he says. "I don't think much of school teachers who can't sing; they need to be able to sing."

Luther has a great concern for teachers of the new faith as well as for evangelical pastors. Things are not going well for most of them.

Elector John starts a visitation program in the parishes of Saxony. Visitors report that the children are simply not praying—or learning either.

Luther works without letup on behalf of the people who have embraced the evangelical faith. In 1526 he publishes *The German Mass and Order of Service.* "Worship," he says on a later occasion, "is hearing God's Word and responding in prayer and songs of praise." Hymn singing by the congregation is certainly part of that.

Luther sings and composes songs—new poems based on psalm texts and hymns of the early church. The first hymn book in the language of the common people appears in 1524, containing just eight songs. Thirty-seven of Luther's hymns have come down to us, including "Out of the Depths I Cry to You" (based on Psalm 130), "Dear Christians, One and All," and "Lord, Keep Us Steadfast in Your Word." Luther has given us hymns for Advent, Christmas, Easter, and Pentecost.

In 1527 he writes the best-known hymn of the Reformation, "A Mighty Fortress Is Our God" (based on Psalm 46), for which Johann Walter provides the music. Luther is pleased at Walter's contribution and says of it later: "I was honored by my good friend Johann Walter, composer of music in Torgau, in 1530."

Facsimile of the original manuscript of "A Mighty Fortress is Our God"

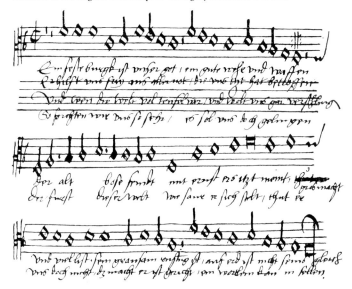

"Good God, what wretchedness I beheld!" Luther says of his own visits. "The common people, especially those who live in the country, have no knowledge whatever of Christian teaching, and unfortunately many pastors are quite incompetent and unfitted for teaching them." It is not five years since Luther had written *To the Councilmen of All Cities in Germany That They Establish and Maintain Christian Schools,* urging public officials everywhere to provide good schools for all the boys and girls. "I cannot praise highly enough the devout and dedicated school teacher who truly nurtures and educates children. Such people are not to be had for money. If I ever had to quit preaching I'd like more than anything else to be a school teacher."

Luther is deeply moved by what he sees on his visits. He thinks hard about how he can be of help: "I will provide a simple course of instruction in the basics of the faith."

Revised edition of the Catechism with cover picture of its author

Title page of the 1534 edition of the complete Bible in German, with printing permit from the Elector of Saxony, John the Constant
Woodcut by Lucas Cranach the Elder

In 1529 Luther writes the Large Catechism for pastors who must preach the evangelical faith, and the Small Catechism to help parents and teachers instruct children. The Small Catechism is divided into five Parts, each dealing with one main aspect of the faith. It is written in question-and-answer form, as in the early church.

Thus, the First Part, dealing with the Ten Commandments, begins:

You shall have no other gods.
What does this mean?
Answer: *We should fear, love, and trust in God above all things.*

Besides the Catechism there is the Bible. Luther continues working long and hard at translating the Old Testament. He gets all the help he can from his friends, especially from Philip Melanchthon on the original Hebrew language. Luther wants all Christians to read the Bible and understand it. In 1534 he completes his translation of the whole Bible. "The Bible is the greatest, the most necessary, the chief thing in Christianity," according to Luther. "They say that letters from the prince should be read three times. Well, God's 'letter'—the Holy Scriptures—should be read 7 x 3 times, indeed 70 x 3 times . . . times without number."

Ulrich Zwingli (1484–1531)—portrait by H. Asper

The Reformation continues to spread all over Europe.

In 1523 Ulrich Zwingli preaches at the cathedral in Zurich. Encouraged by the city fathers, he introduces the Reformation to Switzerland. "We must shape our life according to the Sermon on the Mount," he says. But Zwingli's teachings are not always those of Luther, for example with respect to the Lord's Supper. In 1529 Luther and Zwingli meet at Marburg, in the castle of Landgrave Philip of Hesse, to debate the issue. Zwingli says: "The bread and wine in the Lord's Supper *signify* the body and blood of Christ. What counts is the presence of the Spirit who gives life." But Luther says: "In the Gospel of Mark it says 'Take and eat, this *is* my body!' Bread and wine remain bread and wine, but at the same time they *are* the body and blood of Christ!"

The two are unable to reconcile their differences. So besides the "Evangelical" church of Martin Luther there is now also the church of Ulrich Zwingli, soon to be called "Reformed."

John Calvin (1509–64)—portrait 1564

About 1530 in Geneva, Switzerland, a French preacher by the name of John Calvin experiences a conversion as he is reading the writings of Martin Luther. In 1536 while he is traveling through their city, the people of Geneva prevail on Calvin to stay over and help them institute the Reformation in Geneva. With support from the city officials, Calvin in 1541 sets up a tight system of church government under the motto: "To God alone be the glory." Geneva becomes a theocracy. The life of every citizen is strictly regimented. Church attendance is compulsory. Prohibited under penalty of the law are theater-going, shooting dice, dancing, visiting drinking establishments, and wearing extravagant clothing.

Calvin is a learned biblical scholar and a powerful preacher. For him the congregation is supreme in churchly affairs. Each congregation chooses its own leaders and they interpret the Scriptures. Every member of the parish reads the Bible, not just as a matter of right but as a matter of duty. All Christians have to order their lives by the tenets of the Bible.

Calvin writes a book of Christian instruction called *The Institutes of the Christian Religion* that will have a far-reaching influence. "Man lives only to glorify God," he says. "From even before the beginning of time our lives are laid out by God" (predestination). "God has mercy upon whomever he wills, and he hardens the heart of whomever he wills" (Rom. 9:18). "God's election is firm: no one can change it. Nonetheless every person must try to live a godfearing life."

Calvin's church too is called "Reformed." It spreads rapidly to the Low Countries and France, to England and Scotland. In France the Calvinists are called Huguenots; in England, Puritans; and in Scotland, Presbyterians. Luther's church takes root mainly in Germany and the Scandinavian countries.

"Reformed" worship can be quite plain—no candles, pictures, images, organ, sometimes even no hymns except from the Psalms. Of supreme importance is the Word (Bible and pulpit at the center), and then the deed which follows from it.

Already in the Middle Ages some of the begging monks had put the sermon at the center of worship. Pictured below is the Calvinist "Paradise Church" of Lyon in France 1564. It is meeting in a former city hall converted for worship purposes. A baptismal service is in progress—Painting by Jean Perissin

The vineyard of the Reformation—painted by Lucas Cranach the Younger in 1569 as a memorial to Paul Eber in the City Church of Wittenberg, the "First Church" of the Reformation (see also page 24)

An ongoing concern of the Reformation is to point out the weaknesses of Roman faith and practice. This is often done in paintings. Lucas Cranach the Younger here paints a vine-covered mountain which, by his own explanation, "stands for the Christian church."

On the left side is the vineyard of the old church—on the verge of being destroyed despite all the work going on there. The workers are filling its dried-up well with stones, for their work is the kind of works-righteousness they think God will see and count and reward. But God does not calculate that way.

On the right side is the vineyard of the Reformation, carefully tended by the Reformers (Melanchthon working the well pulley, Luther and others clearing the land). Here no worker supposes that he is earning merit with God. That is why the vineyard flourishes. God does not want our attention focused on righteousness through good works. His rewards are given out of his own pure grace. He gives to all alike, to those who come late into his vineyard (Christians of the Reformation) as well as to those who have worked in it much longer (monks, priests, and bishops of the old church).

The Roman church recognizes that its vineyard is drying up. The Reformation helps it to take stock of itself. At the Council of Trent (1545–63) the pope puts bishops and professors to work thinking anew about the faith, about the doctrines of the church and its need for reform.

In 1563 the Council announces its decisions: The teachings of Luther and Calvin are rejected. There is, however, no more purchasing of indulgences. Sinners are justified by the grace of God, which is given through the merits and suffering of Christ but also through the merits (good works) of the people—though faith, love, and hope are also involved. No bishop may oversee more than one diocese. Priests are now to be educated in seminaries. The sacrifice of the mass remains at the heart of worship. Reaffirmed is the rule that nobody can give a "private interpretation" of Scripture. Only holy mother church can decide on how Scripture is to be understood. The church must remain obedient to its supreme ruler, the pope.

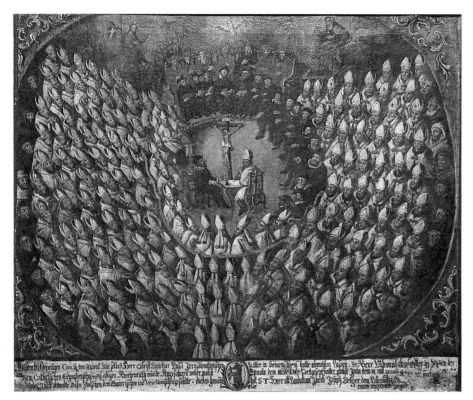

The Council of Trent (1545–63). Many bishops of the old church gather around the cross of Christ
Painting from the Capuchin Monastery at Stans in Switzerland

Ignatius of Loyola, first "general" of the Jesuit order which he founded—1556 portrait attributed to Jacopino del Conte

A Spanish nobleman and ex-soldier named Ignatius of Loyola makes this unconditional obedience to the pope the foundation stone of his Society of Jesus, which is approved by Pope Paul III in 1540. Each member of this Jesuit order, through his daily "spiritual exercises," gives evidence of his strict self-discipline and of his firm obedience to the will of God.

Like Calvin, Ignatius teaches that man is created for the sole purpose of praising, honoring, and serving God, and thereby saving his own soul.

In service to the pope the "soldiers" of Ignatius become the shock troops of the Counter-Reformation.

Ignatius says of the Protestants: "These innovators know how to make their false teachings sound good, but they have made a mess of the Lord's vineyard."

His Jesuit order enjoys immediate success. It soon has branches all over Europe. Members of the Society go out into the world to do their service. They establish schools, teach in universities, and serve as pastor-confessors to Catholic rulers. They carry their mission enterprises to many lands around the world.

While the council is meeting in Trent, Emperor Charles V in June of 1546 joins the pope in an effort to destroy the followers of Martin Luther. The wars of religion begin.

Maurice of Ducal Saxony, a Lutheran, allies himself with the emperor against John Frederick of Electoral Saxony. In the Schmalkald War of 1546–47 the emperor defeats the elector at Mühlberg. John Frederick and Philip of Hesse are both captured. The Protestants are in grave peril.

Charles V still hopes to see the religious questions resolved through a council. For the interim he will concede to the Protestants the right for priests to marry and for laity to receive the sacramental cup—nothing more.

Despite their military defeats, the Protestants will not give in. Maurice suddenly deserts Charles and forces him to flee, never again to return to Germany. In 1555 the new emperor, Charles's brother Ferdinand, concludes with the Protestants the "honorable, definitive, and unconditional" Peace of Augsburg. Both Catholicism and Protestantism are now acceptable, each in its own lands. Neither may infringe the rights of the other. The religion of the ruler will be the religion of the people ("whose the region, his the religion"). Whoever does not like the religion of the land is free to move elsewhere. Protestants are allowed to keep the extensive church holdings which have fallen into their hands.

Luther, however, does not live to see these wars of religion come and go. In 1545 he finishes editing his translation of the complete Bible. His health and strength are failing. On February 18, 1546, Luther dies at Eisleben, the same city where he had been born sixty-three years earlier. He was in town to help mediate a quarrel between the counts of Mansfeld. Luther is buried in the Castle Church at Wittenberg. In the room where he died they found a scrap of paper on which had been scribbled two days before his death the last words he ever wrote: "We are beggars. That is true."

The sketch on the right shows Luther shortly before the year of his death. Philip Melanchthon pasted it inside the back cover of his New Testament and added the last three Latin words: "And though he is dead—he lives."

In one of his last sermons, preached February 7, 1546, Luther has this to say:

If a person earnestly reflects on God's Word in his heart, believes it, and sleeps away and dies in this faith, then he perishes and passes on before he is even aware of death. He has certainly passed from hence, saved by the Word which he contemplates and believes.

Luther at the podium during one of his last lectures in 1545
Sketch by Famulus Reifenstein

ORAVIT, DOCVIT, CHRISTVS, FIT VICTIMA, VICTOR

Das newe Testament.
auffs new zugericht.

I.N.R.I.

Doct: Mart: Luth:

Witeberg.

Gedruckt durch Hans Luffe.
1 5 4 6.

VETVS } testamentum est { FONS }
NOVVM } { LVX }

"In the crucified Christ alone is the true theology and knowledge of God. I can know—I shall know nothing but what this Lord teaches me." This is what Martin Luther believed and preached throughout his life—right up until the day he died. "Christians should be exhorted to be diligent in following Christ, their head, through penalties, death, and hell; and thus be confident of entering into heaven through many tribulations rather than through the false security of peace."

Theses 94 and 95
Ninety-five Theses 1517

No strength of ours can match his might!
We would be lost, rejected.
But now a champion comes to fight,
Whom God himself elected.
You ask who this may be?
The Lord of hosts is he!
Christ Jesus, mighty Lord,
God's only Son, adored.
He holds the field victorious.

Luther and his last elector John Frederick kneel at the foot of Christ's cross. Color woodcut from the 1546 Wittenberg edition of the New Testament, which Luther had himself edited. The top line is in Latin: "He prayed, he taught, Christ the Victor gave himself as victim." At the bottom, also in Latin, are the obviously handwritten words: "The Old and New Testaments are font and light."

Chronology

Church and Empire	Martin Luther
1445 Beginning of book printing	
	1483 Luther is born November 10 in Eisleben to Hans and Margarethe Luther
1484 Papal bull of Innocent VIII condemning witchcraft	1484 Family moves to Mansfeld
1492 Columbus discovers America	
1492–1503 Pope Alexander VI	
1493–1519 Emperor Maximilian	
1498 Savonarola executed in Florence	
	1501 After schooling in Mansfeld, with the Brethren of the Common Life in Magdeburg, and at the St. George's parish school in Eisenach (Cotta house), Luther begins study of liberal arts at Erfurt, enrolling as "Martinus Ludher" of Mansfeld
1502 Frederick the Wise opens new University of Wittenberg	1502 Bachelor of Arts degree
1503–13 Pope Julius II	
	1505 Master of Arts (with honors). Begins study of law. In July enters Black Cloister of the Augustinian Hermits in Erfurt as a novitiate
	1506 Initiation into the order as a monk
	1507 Ordained a priest in April. First mass May 2. In the summer friend John Staupitz, vicar-general of the Augustinian order, assigns Luther to study theology with a view to teaching
	1508 First move to Wittenberg. Lectures in philosophy. Biblical studies under Staupitz
1509–47 King Henry VIII of England	1509 First theological degree in March at Wittenberg. Return to Erfurt in the fall
	1510–11 Journey to Rome on business for the order
	1511 Back in Wittenberg in September. First lectures in theology
	1512 Subprior of Augustinian monastery. Doctor of Theology in October. Succeeds Staupitz as Professor of Biblical Studies at the university
1513–21 Pope Leo X	1513 Begins teaching
1515–47 King Francis I of France	1515 District vicar of the Augustinian cloisters in Thuringia and Meissen
	1517 October 31 letter to Archbishop Albrecht opposing indulgences. *Ninety-five Theses* begins struggle against indulgences
	1518 April disputation in the Augustinian monastery at Heidelberg. Proceedings against Luther begin at Rome in June. In August Melanchthon joins the Wittenberg faculty. Hearing before Cardinal Cajetan at Augsburg in October. In December Frederick the Wise refuses to hand over his professor to Rome
1519–56 Emperor Charles V	1519 January interview with Miltitz at Altenburg. July disputation with Eck at Leipzig: "Councils can err"
	1520 Three Reformation treatises in August-November: *To the Christian Nobility, The Babylonian Captivity,* and *The Freedom of a Christian.* December 10 burning of the decretals and the bull of Pope Leo X at the Elster gate of Wittenberg
1521 Diet of Worms	1521 Excommunication in January. Summons to the Diet of Worms in March. April 17–18 refusal to recant. Edict of Worms against Luther in May. Protective custody of Frederick the Wise at the Wartburg (until March 1522). Fall unrest at Wittenberg. Begins translation of the New Testament in December (published September 1522)

1522–23 The Knights' War
1523 Death of the knights Franz
von Sickingen and Ulrich
von Hutten
1523 Pope Adrian VI
1523–34 Pope Clement VII
1524–25 Peasants' War
1525 Death of Frederick the
Wise. Secularization of the
order in Germany. Battle of
Pavia
1526 Turkish peril. First Diet of
Speyer
1527 Sack of Rome. Marburg the
first evangelical university
1529 Turks besiege Vienna.
Second Diet of Speyer

1530 Diet of Augsburg

1531 State church in England.
Schmalkald League
1532 Truce of Nürnberg
1534–49 Pope Paul III
1534–35 Anabaptist kingdom in
Münster

1540 Pope Paul III recognizes the
Jesuit order
1541 Reformation in Geneva
under John Calvin
(1509–64)
1543 Copernicus: the sun is at
the center of things
1545–63 Council of Trent
1546–47 Schmalkald War

1547 Battle of Mühlberg
1548 Augsburg Interim
1555 Peace of Augsburg

1522 Dissolution of the order's German congregation. "Fanatics" and image-breaking in
Wittenberg. In March Luther returns and preaches eight sermons
1522–23 Reformation in Zurich under Ulrich Zwingli (1484–1531)
1523–24 Luther begins composing hymns. Writes *To the Councilmen of All Cities in Germany
That They Establish and Maintain Christian Schools*

1525 Luther at first favors the peasants, then opposes them. Münzer executed in May. Luther
marries ex-nun Catherine von Bora in June. The church of Saxony reorganizes in
October. Melanchthon begins reforming the schools and university

1526 Princes decide the question of religious affiliation in their territories. *The German Mass*

1529 Evangelicals protest nullification of 1526 decrees; are now called Protestants. Marburg
Colloquy with Zwingli on the Lord's Supper in October. Luther writes the Small and
Large Catechisms
1530 Luther at the Coburg. Melanchthon represents the Reformation. Augsburg Confession
read in June before the Diet. Confutation by Eck. Prohibition of all innovations in the
church

1534 First complete edition of the German Bible

1536–37 Schmalkald Articles

1546 Luther dies at Eisleben February 18. Buried February 22 in the Castle Church at
Wittenberg

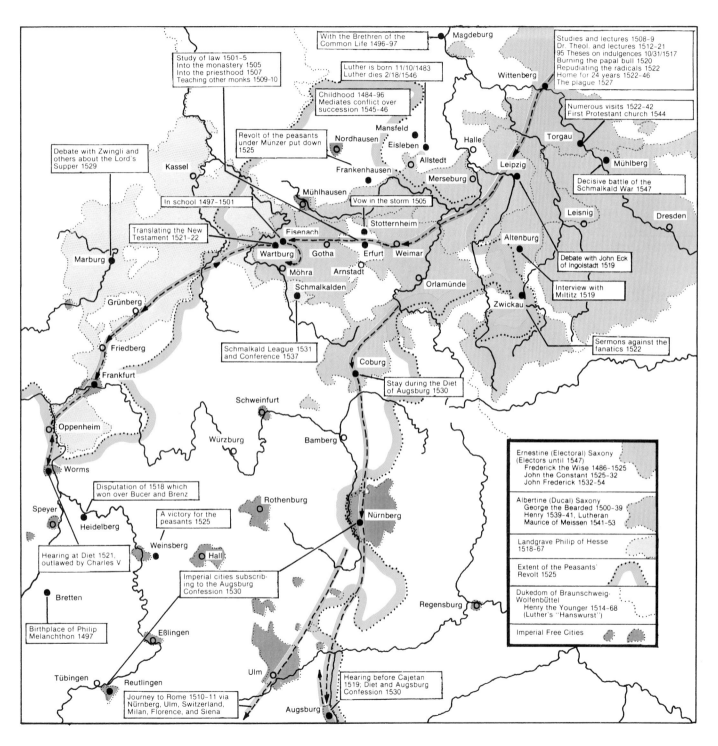

With the Brethren of the Common Life 1496–97

Magdeburg

Studies and lectures 1508-9
Dr. Theol. and lectures 1512–21
95 Theses on indulgences 10/31/1517
Burning the papal bull 1520
Repudiating the radicals 1522
Home for 24 years 1522-46
The plague 1527

Study of law 1501-5
Into the monastery 1505
Into the priesthood 1507
Teaching other monks 1509-10

Luther is born 11/10/1483
Luther dies 2/18/1546

Wittenberg

Childhood 1484-96
Mediates conflict over succession 1545-46

Numerous visits 1522-42
First Protestant church 1544

Mansfeld

Nordhausen

Halle

Torgau

Revolt of the peasants under Münzer put down 1525

Eisleben

Leipzig

Mühlberg

Debate with Zwingli and others about the Lord's Supper 1529

Kassel

Frankenhausen

Allstedt

Merseburg

Decisive battle of the Schmalkald War 1547

In school 1497-1501

Mühlhausen

Vow in the storm 1505

Leisnig

Dresden

Translating the New Testament 1521-22

Eisenach

Stotternheim

Altenburg

Wartburg

Gotha

Erfurt

Weimar

Debate with John Eck of Ingolstadt 1519

Marburg

Möhra

Arnstadt

Orlamünde

Interview with Miltitz 1519

Schmalkalden

Zwickau

Grünberg

Sermons against the fanatics 1522

Schmalkald League 1531 and Conference 1537

Friedberg

Coburg

Frankfurt

Stay during the Diet of Augsburg 1530

Schweinfurt

Oppenheim

Würzburg

Bamberg

Worms

Disputation of 1518 which won over Bucer and Brenz

Rothenburg

Speyer

A victory for the peasants 1525

Nürnberg

Ernestine (Electoral) Saxony
(Electors until 1547)
    Frederick the Wise 1486-1525
    John the Constant 1525-32
    John Frederick 1532-54

Heidelberg

Weinsberg

Hall

Albertine (Ducal) Saxony
    George the Bearded 1500-39
    Henry 1539-41, Lutheran
    Maurice of Meissen 1541-53

Hearing at Diet 1521, outlawed by Charles V

Imperial cities subscribing to the Augsburg Confession 1530

Landgrave Philip of Hesse 1518-67

Bretten

Regensburg

Extent of the Peasants' Revolt 1525

Birthplace of Philip Melanchthon 1497

Eßlingen

Dukedom of Braunschweig-Wolfenbüttel
    Henry the Younger 1514-68
    (Luther's "Hanswurst")

Tübingen

Reutlingen

Ulm

Imperial Free Cities

Journey to Rome 1510-11 via Nürnberg, Ulm, Switzerland, Milan, Florence, and Siena

Hearing before Cajetan 1519; Diet and Augsburg Confession 1530

Augsburg

Acknowledgments

English Quotations

On the following pages certain English quotations derive in whole or in part from the indicated sources:

6—Helmut T. Lehmann, editor, The America Edition of *Luther's Works* (Philadelphia: Fortress Press, 1957–75), 53, 305 [hereafter cited as *LW*].
15—*LW* 48, 47–49; 31, 25–33.
22—Oskar Thulin, editor, *A Life of Luther: Told in Pictures and Narratives by the Reformer and His Contemporaries,* translated by Martin O. Dietrich (Philadelphia: Fortress Press, 1966), p. 17.
23—*LW* 53, 224, 219.
26—*LW* 31, 318.
28—*LW* 44, 127–28; 36, 112–16; 31, 344.
29—Preserved Smith, translator and editor, *Luther's Correspondence and Other Contemporary Letters,* Vol. I: 1507–1521 (Philadelphia: Lutheran Publication Society, 1913), pp. 482–83.
30—*LW* 32, 112.
31—Thulin, p. 68; *LW* 48, 201, 228.
32—*LW* 35, 189, 358.
33—*LW* 45, 65; 48, 391.
40—*LW* 46, 50.
41—*LW* 49, 135; Henry C. Vedder, *The Reformation in Germany* (New York: Macmillan Company, 1914), pp. 433, 439.
44—*LW* 45, 369.
45—Theodore G. Tappert, editor, *The Book of Concord: The Confessions of the Evangelical Lutheran Church* (Philadelphia: Fortress Press, 1959), pp. 338, 342.
51—Thulin, p. 127.
52—*LW* 31, 33; *Lutheran Book of Worship* (Minneapolis: Augsburg Publishing Company; Philadelphia: Board of Publication, Lutheran Church in America, 1978), 229.

Photo Credits

Archiv für Kunst und Geschichte, Berlin 34–35; Biblioteca Apostolica Vaticana, Rome 21B; Bibliothèque Nationale, Paris 8BL; Erzbetei St. Peter, Salzburg 22T; Fürstlich Waldburg Zeil'sches Gesamtarchiv, Leutkirch 39T, 40B; Galleria Borghese, Rome 29T; Germanisches Nationalmuseum, Nürnberg 4, 14T, 25T, 31B; Gutenberg Museum, Mainz 10T; Herzog Anton Ulrich Museum, Braunschweig 11B; Kunsthistorisches Museum, Vienna 8T; Helmuth Nils Loose 8BR, 9BR, 14BL & BR, 18, 20T, 24, 26B, 33B, 36B, 41, 43, 46, 47, 48–49, 50; Lutherhalle, Wittenberg, title page, 10B, 16B, 21T, 23, 25B, 27B, 28R, 29B, 36T, 38T, 42B, 45B, 51, 52; Melanchthon Museum, Bretten 2; National Gallery, London 8BL; Universitätsbibliothek, Basel 33T; Zeitbild Archiv Maiwald, Garmisch-Partenkirchen 5, 6, 7, 9T, 11T, 12B, 17, 19T, 22B, 32T, 38B, 39B, 42T, 44, 45T.

Map 55 Karl Hartmann, Sulz/Neckar

This book is a translation by Edward A. Cooperrider of an initial version (different in minor details) of *Reformation—Martin Luther. Ein Sachbilderbuch zur Kirchengeschichte,* Copyright © 1983 by Verlag Ernst Kaufmann, D–7630 Lahr, Federal Republic of Germany and Christophorus-Verlag, D–7800 Freiburg, Federal Republic of Germany.

English translation copyright © 1983 by Fortress Press

Library of Congress Cataloging in Publication Data

Steinwede, Dietrich.
  Reformation : a picture story of Martin Luther.

  Translation of: Reformation : Martin Luther : ein Sachbilderbuch zur Kirchengeschichte.
  1. Luther, Martin, 1483-1546. 2. Reformation—Biography. 3. Reformation. 4. Reformation in art. 5. Art, Renaissance. I. Title.
BR325.S71613 1983   284.1′092′4   82-49055
ISBN 0-8006-1710-X

9757K82 Printed in the Federal Republic of Germany 1–1710